FINDING PEACE
THROUGH PRAYER

INTO
THE
DEEP

DAN BURKE

Cover design: Dan Donohue
Interior: Finer Points Productions

ISBN: 978-1-942611-51-6 (hard cover)
ISBN: 978-1-942611-53-0 (soft cover)

Library of Congress Cataloging-in-Publication Data
Names: Burke, Dan, 1965- author.
Title: Into the deep : finding peace through prayer / Dan Burke.
Description: North Palm Beach : Beacon Publishing, 2016.
Identifiers: LCCN 2016027340| ISBN 9781942611516 (hardcover) | ISBN 9781942611530 (softcover) | ISBN 9781942611615 (ebook)
Subjects: LCSH: Prayer—Catholic Church. | Catholic Church—Doctrines.
Classification: LCC BV210.3 .B86 2016 | DDC 248.3/2—dc23
                                      2016027340

Printed in the United States of America [1]

CONTENTS

FOREWORD

Prayer is difficult, joyful, challenging, and life-changing. The journey into prayer, into the heart of God, is the reason we were made; it is the reason God brought us into existence.

You have a defining moment before you on this journey. What you are about to read is clear, powerful, and applicable to every Catholic who knows there is something more to life; every Catholic whose heart yearns for something more; every Catholic who wants to know God better.

This defining moment exists because God has brought this book to you. He is reaching out to you again, seeking to draw you near. If you answer the call with all that you are, God will match your commitment, and he will not only meet you where you are, he will take you to a place that you never knew existed, a place where two hearts—God's and yours—beat as one.

This place, this journey, this battle is worth every ounce of effort you can give it. It is worth everything you own, everything you aspire to be, everything you are. If you commit, persevere, and embrace this journey, you will know the life that Jesus has promised, a life of peace and joy that cannot be taken away by the trials of this world.

Lean in, persevere, learn, practice, fight, embrace, rejoice— God is with you on this journey of prayer.

Matthew Kelly

INTRODUCTION

WHY PRAY?

Some time ago my youngest brother, who is a bit baffled by my faith, asked me an important question: "Dan, do you pray every day?"

I replied, "Yes."

He asked, "*Every, every* day?"

Again I said, "Yes."

He then asked again but with an emphasis in his tone that reflected some measure of disbelief and a demand for an absolutely honest answer. "*Every, every, every* day?"

A light went on in my head, and I realized what he was really asking me. "Dennis, you don't understand—I don't pray because I am holy; I pray because I am not." I continued, "I am not capable of living a life without God. This is why I pray *every, every, every* day."

The idea of my own incapacity to live even a single day without prayer is not new or unique to me. One of the most oft-quoted sayings in the history of Christianity is St. Augustine's line in his *Confessions*, ". . . our heart is restless until it rests in you." The reason this is cited so often, even more than a thousand years after it was written, is that it rings true across all cultures and throughout all time. Any heart open to God says "yes" when it hears this beautiful expression. We know in the depths of our being that this is true. The reason it is true is revealed in the full quote, which reads, "You have made us for yourself, O Lord, and our heart is restless until it rests in You."

St. Augustine recognizes that our hearts are restless to the degree that we fail to orient all that we are to God. Our restlessness comes from a disorientation of our hearts. To the degree that we give ourselves to God in prayer, the restlessness will begin to subside. To the degree that we give ourselves to God, we fulfill the purpose of our existence; we know union with God and thus know the peace and joy that enable us to face and overcome whatever comes our way.

If your heart is restless like mine, there is a path to peace and joy available to you. This path can only be found in and through prayer.

Beyond the central cry of our hearts to God, prayer is far more essential to our eternal salvation than many suppose. Human beings need air, water, and food to live. Without any one of these three basic elements, we will eventually die. Similarly, the sacraments of the Church, especially the Eucharist and penance, are as spiritually essential to us as the air we breathe. Without the sacraments—without air—nothing else matters.

In this analogy, prayer and the life of virtue are comparable to food and water. With air, or the sacraments, essential for life, prayer and virtue keep us nourished and healthy. In terms of food, if we don't have all the proper nutrients, we can suffer disease and death. So it is with prayer and virtue. The daily nourishment of prayer that flows out of our sacramental participation is the life-blood of the abundant life promised to us by Jesus.

So, air is not enough—without prayer, we will not be sufficiently nourished to find the "life abundant" that Christ promises us. Without prayer we will inevitably drift from the sacraments and become mired in sin and narcissism; we will be distracted from the most important things in life and our ability to hear and respond to God will become dulled. With the absence of these essential elements, we will find ourselves leaving the narrow path to heaven and stepping onto the wide road to destruction that Jesus described in the seventh chapter of St. Matthew's Gospel.

Here's what St. Bonaventure said regarding what a heart committed to prayer can expect from his or her exercise of faith:

[B]y prayer the soul is cleansed from sin, replenished with charity, confirmed in faith, strengthened, and refreshed in spirit. Prayer establishes the inward man, brings peace to the heart, knows the truth, conquers temptations, expels sorrow, renews the senses, stirs up languishing virtue, puts to flight tepidity, and scours the rust of vices. In prayer, the quick sparkles of celestial desires are incessantly sent forth, from the burning coals of divine love. The privileges of prayer are rare, the prerogatives admirable. Prayer unlocks the gates of heaven, manifests divine secrets, and always finds free access to the ears of God.

The saints over all time have echoed an endless list of the benefits of prayer. A holy Franciscan friar named Johannes de Caulibus compiled this list:

If you would:

- Patiently endure adversity . . . be a person of prayer
- Overcome tribulation and temptations . . . be a person of prayer
- Trample upon your perverse inclinations . . . be a person of prayer
- Know the deceits of Satan, and avoid them . . . be a person of prayer
- Live joyfully in the work of God . . . be a person of prayer
- Peacefully endure the way of labor and affliction . . . be a person of prayer
- Exercise yourself in a spiritual course . . . be a person of prayer

- Not walk according to the desires of the flesh . . . be a person of prayer
- Put to flight your vain or troubling thoughts . . . be a person of prayer
- Nourish your soul with holy thoughts . . . be a person of prayer
- Cultivate in your heart good desires, fervor, and devotion . . . be a person of prayer
- Strengthen and establish your heart and constant purpose in the service of God . . . be a person of prayer
- Uproot vice and sin and plant virtue in your soul . . . be a person of prayer[1]

The bottom line? If you want something to go right in life, pray! God didn't make us for the purpose of abandoning us to meaningless toil and suffering. The reality is that he wants to work with us in life so that we can know a kind of abundance that cannot be known outside of a relationship with him.

1 Daniel Burke, ed., *Finding God through Meditation: St. Peter of Alcantara* (Steubenville, Ohio: Emmaus Road, 2015).

ONE

YOUR DESIRE FOR GOD, GOD'S DESIRE FOR YOU

Growing in prayer is an exciting adventure! There is nothing more fulfilling in life than deepening your relationship with God. Your desire to begin to pray or deepen your prayer life is one that comes from God himself. This is good news because as St. Paul reveals in Philippians 1:6, when God begins a work in us, he will "bring it to completion."

Said another way, your desire *is* the promise of God. It is the unmistakable evidence of his work already under way in your heart *and* the promise that *he will give you whatever you need* to realize the fulfillment of your desire as long as you persevere.

As the prologue of the *Catechism of the Catholic Church* reveals, we were created with this desire and for an eternal relationship of love with God:

God, infinitely perfect and blessed in himself, in a plan of sheer goodness freely created man to make him share in his own blessed life. For this reason, at every time and in every place, God draws close to man. He calls man to seek him,

10/31/2018 6:29 PM PDT — The fact that I want more of God is a sign that he is already working in me

to know him, to love him with all his strength. He calls together all men, scattered and divided by sin, into the unity of his family, the Church. To accomplish this, when the fullness of time had come, God sent his Son as Redeemer and Savior. In his Son and through him, he invites men to become, in the Holy Spirit, his adopted children and thus heirs of his blessed life. (*CCC*, 1)

A powerful way to absorb this beautiful passage is to personalize it and say it out loud. Here's how it reads from this perspective. To get the full import of this astounding reality, read it slowly out loud:

God, infinitely perfect and blessed in himself, in a plan of sheer goodness freely created *me* to *draw and empower me* to share in his own blessed life.

For this reason, at every time and in every place, God draws close to *me*.

He calls *me* to seek him, to know him, to love him with all *my* strength.

He calls *me* together with all men, scattered and divided by sin, into the unity of his family, the Church.

To accomplish this, when the fullness of time had come, God sent his Son to redeem and save *me*.

In his Son and through him, he invites *me* to become,

in the Holy Spirit, his adopted *child* and thus *heir* of his blessed life.

Understanding, embracing, and living the reality revealed by St. John that "he first loved us" (1 John 4:19) is the first step in beginning—or beginning again—in prayer. This first step is also echoed in another beautiful section of the *Catechism*, which speaks of God's desire for us in prayer:

> The wonder of prayer is revealed beside the well where we come seeking water: there, Christ comes to meet every human being. It is he who first seeks us and asks us for a drink. Jesus thirsts; his asking arises from the depths of God's desire for us. Whether we realize it or not, prayer is the encounter of God's thirst with ours. *God thirsts that we may thirst for him.* (CCC, 2560; emphasis added)
>
> Paradoxically our prayer of petition is a response to the plea of the living God: "They have forsaken me, the fountain of living waters, and hewn out cisterns for themselves, broken cisterns that can hold no water!" Prayer is the response of faith to the free promise of salvation and also a response of love to the thirst of the only Son of God. (*CCC*, 2561)

Have you ever considered the reality that God thirsts for you? At the Last Supper, the final gathering of Jesus and his disciples, Jesus revealed this same important truth in another way. He said to the apostles, "I have earnestly desired to eat this Passover with *you* before I suffer" (Luke 22:15; emphasis added). Mystical writers of the Church reveal that the "you" in this passage includes the apostles, but it also is directed to *you.* Jesus longs to commune with *you* in the Eucharist at Mass and he longs to commune with *you* in prayer.

The God of the universe created you for the sole purpose of fulfilling this longing—to be with you, to commune with you, to die for your sins so that you could be eternally reconciled to him and drawn into a relationship of love that is more important than any relationship you will ever have in this life.

The second step to beginning or beginning again in prayer is to begin praying! This is why at the outset of this book I strongly encourage you, if you do not already have a set time to pray daily, to make a firm decision and begin praying *today*. It is as simple as setting aside ten to fifteen minutes to prayerfully read and put the ideas in this book into practice.

This firm decision should be one that reflects a steadfast orientation to a lifelong pursuit of God in prayer. It should be a lasting determination that no matter how hard or easy that pursuit of prayer is, we will continue to fight. No matter how many times we fail, we will, by the grace of God, begin again. In our determined pursuit we can know that God is even more firm in his pursuit of us and that he will help us every time we fall, as long as we desire his help and choose to get back up. He gave the very life of his Son for us—would he withhold anything else?

Before we jump into how to overcome difficulties in prayer and other wisdom about how to have a rich experience of God in prayer, there is a simple and practical approach that has transformed the lives of millions: Discovery Prayer. Discovery Prayer is a modern name for an ancient but ever new practice called Lectio Divina (a Latin phrase that means "Divine Reading"); this practical method will build a strong foundation for an ongoing prayer life.

Beginning to pray even before we completely understand prayer is the best way to learn, because actually praying is more important than acquiring abstract knowledge about prayer by merely reading about it. No one learns to swim by sitting by the side of a pool and talking about swimming or watching others swim. It is true that once you master the basics, you could spend days on important stroke technique, water balance, and breathing. However, all good swimming courses begin *in the water* because so much cannot be learned without the actual experience of immersion. We must learn as we do in order to make real progress. So let's jump in!

TWO

DISCOVERY PRAYER

n my interaction with thousands of God seekers over the years, one of the most common questions I receive is, "What is the best way to learn to pray?" In my studies I have explored just about every modern and ancient practice and have come to appreciate the great blessings provided through many other forms. However, Discovery Prayer stands out because it has a built-in approach to prayer, which if practiced with wisdom will likely lead to depths of prayer and encounters with God that are life-changing.

This form of communion with God is an approach to prayer and Scripture reading practiced by mystics, monks, religious sisters, priests, deacons, laypeople, and saints for thousands of years (even before the time of Christ). Even so, the approach is ever new to each person because God meets each of us uniquely in prayer in the way that we specifically need him to. I have given this approach a modern name because it helps to reveal what will happen as we practice this kind of prayer. The simple reality is that if we draw near to God in prayer, we will *discover* his presence in our lives. We will *discover* his love. We will *discover* his peace. We will *discover* who we really are and our ultimate calling and purpose.

About a thousand years ago a monk named Guigo illustrated the idea of Discovery Prayer by using the image of steps on a ladder to heaven. Here's a brief summary of each rung of the ladder of Discovery Prayer. Later in this book, we will dig deeper and spend more time walking through each step of this approach to prayer. If you begin now, even if you struggle a bit, you will be better prepared for what is to come:

Reading: Performing an attentive, slow, leisurely, and repetitious reading of a short passage of the Bible

Reflecting: Making an effort to prayerfully engage with the meaning of the passage and to consider how it may apply to your life circumstances

Responding: Conversing with God about the passage

Resting: Allowing yourself to rest and remain absorbed in the words of God; allowing or inviting the Holy Spirit to draw you more deeply into his presence through what you've read

Resolving: Allowing the encounter with God to permeate your day, causing you to draw near to him through his self-revelation and unique call to you to participate with him in the redemption of the world

To jump into Discovery Prayer at this point, simply set aside ten minutes a day and begin to practice the easiest of these steps—reading and reflecting. The rest of this book will be dedicated to helping you gain a deeper understanding of this approach to prayer and how you can overcome common challenges you will encounter. We will also dig a bit deeper to reveal perspectives that will help you overcome difficulties and continue to make progress well after you have finished the book.

PREPARATION FOR DISCOVERY PRAYER

Before we take a deeper dive into Discovery Prayer, it is important to establish a few key elements that will help you make sure and steady progress. Each element is preceded by the word *sacred* because when we encounter something sacred, we know that it is very important or special.

Most of us have been to war memorials, cemeteries, or churches and have experienced moments when we have sensed the sacred nature of the place. We intuitively understand that there is a reason that we don't hold volleyball tournaments or have cookouts in cemeteries or play Ping-Pong on the altars of our churches. We recognize that this sacred ground is set apart for just one purpose: to give the highest possible honor to those worthy of it. This "setting apart as special" is what the word *sacred* means, except that it goes one step further when it comes to prayer and our commitments to God.

When we use the word *sacred* for our commitment regarding time, what we mean is that we consecrate or dedicate a portion of our time *to* God and only *for* God. We make a solemn promise that this time is his and that we will never (within reason) use it for anything other than the purpose that we have set aside for it.

This setting aside as sacred is similar to the sanctuary in any Catholic church. The sanctuary is that area where the altar and the tabernacle are. It is the most holy and special place in a Catholic church and should be treated as such. It is never to be walked in or through lightly without acknowledging the presence of the Lord. It is never to be used for any purpose other than the Mass. In this way, when we call something sacred, it is special and set apart purely for God.

Another perspective that might be helpful is that when something is consecrated as sacred, it can never again be used for another purpose. As an example, what would happen if we gave a hundred dollars to a homeless shelter and then returned a week later to ask for it back? Of course, the people who run the shelter would be baffled and troubled by our actions. How would your friends react if they knew you had done that? They would be horrified and concerned about your mental or spiritual state. Why? Because you gave that money away for an important and significant need: feeding those who wouldn't be fed if you didn't give. Similarly, when we consecrate something to God, we are giving something to him that we would not ever dare take back.

However, it is far easier to leave a single gift in the hands of a recipient than it is to give that same gift on a daily basis. So it is with prayer. One way we can overcome this challenge is through a conscious act of faith—a prayer of real commitment to God.

This sacred commitment is a very serious promise we make to God regarding our desire to give him a special space in our lives, a kind of altar in our souls. The rite to dedicate a church and altar in the Catholic Church is about ten thousand words long. This provides some perspective on how important it is to properly dedicate places of sacred worship. This importance is marked by the power of ritual, a special ceremony that requires specific actions and prayers. The power of the ritual imbues all involved with the transcendent nature of the dedication and makes a deep and lasting impression on them. To the degree that their hearts are properly oriented to the work and presence of God in their dedication, their participation in the ritual forever impacts the way each participant treats this sacred space. So it can be with how we make our commitments to God.

We don't need ten thousand words or prayers and a priest or bishop, but we can show the depth of our commitment to prayer by expressing an appropriate level of solemnity and seriousness. This kind of action is very powerful for the soul and will help us stay on track when we struggle. To help you to make your own sacred commitment, after reviewing the three elements necessary for success in prayer, you'll find a prayer you can use to dedicate the sanctuary of your soul to God.

THREE

ESSENTIAL ELEMENTS FOR PROGRESS IN PRAYER

J ust like a church is not a church without an altar, a few essential elements are required for your progress in prayer. These elements embody the universal secrets of success in prayer that you will find in the lives of every person who has been serious about growing spiritually. In modern business terms, these are called "best practices." Those who are successful in business learn from the success of others. In the same way, those who make serious progress in the spiritual life always pursue and learn from the spiritual best practices of those around them and those who have gone before them—the saints. In the case of prayer, these three essential elements reflect the very best practices of those who have known profound success in their spiritual lives. Each of these sacred elements in your soul must be pursued, developed, and fiercely protected in order for your prayer life to mature and deepen from the beginning to the end of your life, when you'll see God face-to-face.

Sacred Time: As with any serious attempt to progress in the spiritual life, prayer requires time and patience. There has never been anyone who experienced significant progress in prayer without a *daily* commitment to meet with God.

When you begin, commit to at least ten or fifteen minutes every day. The best way to do this is to schedule your prayer time at the beginning of each day, *before* you schedule anything else. Trying to squeeze prayer into a busy schedule will always result in busyness edging prayer out of that schedule. View your prayer time as sacred and nonnegotiable. Once you choose the time, promise God that you will protect it and treat it as a priority.

As you begin this new adventure of prayer, the Discovery Prayer process might feel a bit mechanical until you master the approach and develop a natural rhythm. If you're like most people, you will encounter distractions, and you won't fully understand how to use the method well. This is where patience comes in. Later we will discuss specific strategies for minimizing the impact of distractions.

In the beginning, it is important to keep expectations realistic (you won't be levitating in mystical ecstasy the first time you sit down) and to keep things as simple as possible. There are no prayer police who will be looking over your shoulder making sure you exercise perfection in your practice. There is no need to worry about the details or obsess over the method. Instead, simply and peacefully seek Christ in and through the Scriptures. He is waiting for you there and will be delighted to lead you into a continually deepening relationship with him. With that in mind, let's talk about how best to prepare for our time with him.

Sacred Space: Jesus instructed his followers to pray in secret in their "inner room" (see Matthew 6:6). It is ideal to create a space dedicated to prayer and nothing else. You might think this is not feasible, but it only requires a few feet of space.

You can use any suitable surface for a favorite icon, candle, or holy image; for example, a quiet, unused corner space with a small shelf. One person I know crawls into her closet under the hanging clothing to pray sitting on pillows (no candles allowed in there!). My first prayer space was a very simple combination of a windowsill, an icon, a candle, and a small bench. The entire space took up less than four square feet. Your space need not be large or complicated, just protected and set aside for your use during prayer.

Be sure that your prayer space is peaceful and devoid of anything that might draw your attention or distract you (computers, phones, TV, iThings, etc.). This space may include special lighting, candles, or incense to create an atmosphere that fosters calm and peace and signals your mind, body, and soul—through your senses—that it is time to pray. The presence of icons and other visual aids for meditation helps make this signal very clear and effectual.

Just as you set aside a special time for God, it is important to dedicate this special space to use just for your time with him. The effect over time is that you will enter this sacred space and will naturally be drawn to prayer. This is one of the least known but effective secrets of a profound prayer life. Building the habit of prayer includes the environment, and its overall effect will be to help you to pray.

Sacred Attention: Once your environment is properly prepared, make sure your posture is conducive to peaceful prayer and reading, recognizing that you are entering into the presence of God. Your posture should be the same as if you were with Christ in the flesh or before him in Eucharistic adoration. Simplicity is key. There's no need to overemphasize posture the way non-Christian Eastern meditation practices often do. Authentic prayer in the Christian tradition may be helped by a method and by posture, but it is never enslaved to them, and it is never contingent upon them. We can actually pray anyplace, anytime, and in just about any posture. However, certain postures are more conducive to remaining awake and attentive and to prayerfully reading Scripture. If you are tired in the morning, praying while lying on your back is not likely to result in anything but falling asleep. As well, certain postures are more appropriate to being in the presence of God than others.

Now it is time to turn your heart to God. Begin to breathe slowly and deeply, focusing on simple attentiveness to Jesus as you seek to turn to him in Scripture. There is nothing magical about breathing slowly, but it gives you a way of slowing down and relaxing a bit and beginning to shift your focus away from all things other than what God desires to reveal to you in his Word. When you first begin developing a prayer habit, you need all the help you can get. Thus, a special time, special place, your posture, and the way you breathe all help to orient your heart to the work of focusing your attention on God.

If your mind wanders—and it will until the day you die— don't allow for frustration or self-condemnation; simply and *gently* bring your attention back to God and the text. It is important to note that, unlike non-Christian forms of Eastern meditation that seek to empty the mind or manage thoughts, authentic Christian prayer always seeks to *fill* the mind with God, either with images or thoughts or by silently gazing on him. This gentle but purposeful effort will yield a constant aiming and re-aiming of your heart and mind toward him and his Word.

FOUR

MAKING A SOLEMN COMMITMENT TO GOD

Now that you understand the basic steps and the essential elements of prayer, it is time to make an informed, purposeful, and meaningful commitment to God.

There is a reason that, if we are wise, we slow down when we are asked to sign our name to any document that is legally binding. We instinctively know that we should be careful and take what we are doing seriously. This kind of consideration and care is common with contracts, and it should be much more serious when we make commitments to God. So as we desire God to meet us in prayer, we must fully embrace all that will be necessary to experience this union with him, and that embrace must include serious consideration and concern. Even so, we may not know how to do this on a practical level. To remedy this lack of familiarity, I've outlined a simple approach to making a solemn commitment to God.

The first step is to determine the exact promise you intend to make. Another best practice in business, as well as in the lives of the saints, is to write out important commitments. Those who are most successful at reaching their goals ensure that those goals are realistic, clear, concrete, specific, and time bound. You can write your pledge in the form of a letter to God that might look something like this:

Dear God, I know that without you, I can accomplish nothing of meaning in this life, and with you, as you have promised in your Word, I can accomplish anything you have called me to do. I also recognize that to be with you, to love you as you deserve and as I desire, I must learn to pray and to purposefully pursue a relationship with you, first in the sacraments, and second through prayer. Here is my promise to you:

I will develop a sacred space in my home suitable for daily prayer. I will purchase an icon that draws my heart to you. I will also find a bench or chair and a candle. I will do this within the next thirty days.

I will dedicate sacred time to you and, by your grace, I will get up fifteen minutes earlier every day, committing the time between 7:10 a.m. and 7:25 a.m. to you. I promise that I will never use that time for anything else unless there is a legitimate emergency. I will work hard to give special emphasis to this effort over the next thirty days so I can make it a habit. I will begin this new adventure in prayer with you this coming Monday morning.

I will devote sacred attention to you during this time of prayer. I promise to focus my attention on you as best as I possibly can by reading Scripture using the Discovery Prayer approach.

The next step, with your written commitment in hand, is to visit your parish, a monastery, or a shrine. The best possible option is before the Blessed Sacrament exposed for adoration. In some of these cases, you might have to ask your priest to allow for your brief time of self-dedication, depending on the schedule of exposition, benediction, and other prayers or music that he might have planned. When scheduled times of adoration are long, this won't be a challenge at all. As well, your priest might even be willing to pray a special blessing for you and your commitment.

Once you are as calm and peaceful as possible, simply acknowledge that Christ is with you. Pray in this (or some similar) way:

In the name of the Father, and of the Son, and of the Holy Spirit.

Jesus, I know you are with me. Thank you for allowing me to acknowledge your presence. Thank you for being here with me now, for drawing me to prayer, and for promising me that you will help me grow ever more deeply in my relationship with you.

Then you might offer a traditional prayer to the Holy Spirit:

Come, Holy Spirit, fill the hearts of your faithful, and kindle in them the fire of your love.

Send forth your Spirit and they shall be created, and you shall renew the face of the earth.

O God, by the light of the Holy Spirit you have taught the hearts of your faithful. In the same Spirit, help us to know what is truly right and always to rejoice in your consolation. We ask this through Christ our Lord. Amen.

Begin your time of promise with a few moments of silence. Gaze upon Jesus in the Blessed Sacrament and know that he is looking back at you in love. He loved you enough to bring you into existence and to die for your sins, and now, more than ever before, you are responding to that love.

Pray (out loud if possible, or whispered if others are present):

Lord Jesus, I come before you now to answer your call to follow you. What I offer you now I offer because I love you and I know what you have done for me, and I want to respond to your gift of love to me in the best way that I can. Accordingly, I solemnly commit to [list your prayer commitments].

After making your commitments, allow for a moment of silence in Christ's presence.

> *In making these solemn commitments to you, I recognize that my will is not sufficient to achieve what I desire and what you have asked of me. As I seek to give myself to you in this way, I beg for the graces from you to orient my heart, my mind, and my life to you in this special way. I affirm in faith that you have initiated and desire this work in me and that you will be "faithful to complete it"—to give me all I need to love you as you deserve and to know what it means to live a life of love and peace in you.*

After this prayer, remain before Jesus again in silence. Look at him and allow him to look at you in the depths of your being. Give your heart to him. You are his precious child, and he delights in your desire to follow him. "And I am sure that he who began a good work in you will bring it to completion at the day of Jesus Christ" (Philippians 1:6).

FIVE

STEP-BY-STEP INTO THE PRESENCE OF GOD

Now it's time for us to explore Discovery Prayer at a deeper level. This will give you the tools you need to further increase your success as you pursue God. If you followed my advice and jumped in and began praying immediately, you should be more than ready for a deeper look at Discovery Prayer. At the end of each step, I'll provide key questions to help you focus in prayer in order to guide your thinking and engagement along the way.

STEP ONE: READING

The first step begins as you enter your sacred space. Be sure you leave behind anything that might distract you during this time you have dedicated to God. It is important to avoid engaging with technology right before you pray, as this tends to stir the mind and cause distractions.

Before you begin reading, greet the Lord. In my prayer every morning, I simply light three candles, bow my head, and say,

"Good morning, Lord." Then I continue, "Glory be to you, Father; to you, Son; and to you, Holy Spirit."

Next, slowly and gently pray an opening prayer out loud. As you pray, maintain a pace that is slower than normal and peaceful. Consider the meaning of each word as you pray as you say it. Ensure you are directing your attention to God as you pray. Changing the pace of how you normally read or talk will signal to your body and mind that the activity you are about to begin is different and special. Eventually, this conditioning will work in your favor to help you maintain a habit of prayerful attention.

> *O God, come to my assistance; O Lord, make haste to help me.*
>
> *Glory be to the Father, to the Son, and to the Holy Spirit, as it was in the beginning, is now, and will be forever. Amen.*
>
> *Thank you for your love and your grace and for allowing me to be here with you to pray. Thank you for your presence in my soul and for desiring to be with me now.*

Next, begin with an attentive, slow reading of a short passage of Scripture in the Gospels. Why the Gospels? There are a number of reasons, the first of which is that the person and work of Jesus are what the Gospels are all about. If we want to get to know Jesus, there is no better place to do so than in the Gospels.

Each of the Gospels tells the story of Jesus' life from a unique perspective. Here is a summary of each and an outline of how it follows Jesus' life and sacrifice on our behalf:

- **St. Matthew's Gospel** is the story of Jesus, the Messiah (or "Christ"), King of the Jews, and his "kingdom of heaven." This Gospel is written to Jewish converts of Palestine and focuses on Christ's fulfillment of Old Testament prophecies and the Mosaic law. Matthew references more than sixty passages of the Old Testament in his revelation of Jesus as the long-awaited Messiah.
- **St. Mark's Gospel** is a brief and fast-paced summary focused on Jesus' extraordinary works on earth as the Son of God. It is written to Gentiles, particularly Roman Gentile converts. St. Mark reveals the emotions and affections of both Christ and those he engages. He gives interesting details of Jesus' gestures, looks, and words. He shows Christ's anger, love, pity, grief, and wonder. At the same time Mark records the deep impression Christ's words and miracles had on his followers, and it grows in intensity as Jesus approaches the cross. St. Mark's Gospel is arranged to be easily read, remembered, and spread.
- **St. Luke's Gospel** begins through the eyes of Mary. This Gospel of mercy provides the account of Jesus' life in

journalistic style and chronological order, written to establish believers in the teachings of Jesus. St. Luke includes a great deal of detail in his Gospel, making it the longest of the four, and the longest book in the New Testament.

- **St. John's Gospel** breaks with the basic outlines of Matthew, Mark, and Luke and is thematic and symbolic in nature. John records signs emphasizing the deity of Jesus Christ so the reader may believe in Jesus and find life in him. John's Gospel takes a different approach to Jesus' life. Instead of beginning with his birth (like Matthew and Luke) or earthly ministry (like Mark), John starts with Jesus' work at the beginning of creation.

It's a good practice to choose the Gospel passage from the Mass of the day or the Mass of the upcoming Sunday. This helps keep your prayer rooted in the source and summit of our faith, the Eucharist. Another helpful approach is to take each of the four Gospels, one at a time, and pray through them over the course of months (or years). You can start with whichever Gospel sounds most interesting to you.

The key is not to rush. The goal is not to finish a particular portion of Scripture—or even to finish the steps laid out in Discovery Prayer—but to purposefully delve into the depths of any passage that will draw your heart and mind to God. Said another way, this method is meant to orient your mind and heart to God, and you can set aside the method when this happens during any given time in prayer.

As you begin, you might also follow a beautiful tradition and trace the sign of the cross on the Scriptures, kiss the cross you traced, and then begin to read very slowly and gently—out loud —seeking to absorb the words themselves along with any related ideas and images that surface from each word. Reading aloud is ideal because it stimulates your senses and your body in general (your hearing, your vocal cords, your mouth) and thus helps you to focus on God and better avoid distractions. It also helps you to slow down and increase mental engagement.

When a particular passage or word strikes you, pause to consider it more fully. As you pause, you will then naturally move into step two, reflecting. If you don't seem to progress in the way suggested by this method, simply continue reading slowly and even reread the passage.

As a general rule, each selected short (as short as possible) portion of Scripture should be read aloud slowly three times before you move on to the next section. Each of us moves at our own pace, however. The goal is not to mechanically execute the method, but to honor and seek God.

This first step, reading slowly, cannot be overemphasized. When you read at your natural or normal pace, you are reading for information. But this prayerful reading is meant to help you encounter Jesus, listen to his voice, and follow his lead. If you read at your normal pace, you will miss the quiet call of God to venture into deeper waters.

 Key Questions for Reading: What does the Bible text say in itself? What did the author intend?

STEP TWO: REFLECTING

In this second step, you engage with the details, words, places, visual images, attitudes, and insights of the passage, seeking to fully absorb and understand it and then apply it to your own life.

Gently and peacefully ponder what you have read, visualizing it and listening carefully for the Holy Spirit's prompting or guidance. Look for the deeper spiritual meanings of the words as you place yourself in a Gospel scene as one of the participants, or simply hear God speaking directly to you as you read the words.

What does it mean to place yourself in the Gospel scene? Use your imagination to see yourself as a particular person in the setting or as part of the crowd surrounding the scene. For instance, you might see yourself as the Samaritan woman at the well who meets and talks with Jesus, to the astonishment of his disciples, in the fourth chapter of St. John's Gospel. You might put yourself in the place of the prodigal son in the fifteenth chapter of St. Luke's Gospel. You might consider the temperature, the movement of the wind, the clothing of the people, the dust, the smells, the heat, and the look of the surrounding elements. The more you can slow down to consider these things, the more you will be able to enter into the passage and engage with the life-changing truths presented, and the more you will discover about yourself and about God's love and calling for you.

Regardless of the passages you choose, don't rack your brain or exert extreme intellectual effort as you reflect. Simply engage and allow the words and related images to penetrate your heart and mind, and follow wherever God leads you through the text.

It is important to avoid a scientific or excessively intellectual examination of Scripture as if you were preparing to teach a course or explain it to someone else. Instead your goal is to listen carefully for God's leading. The prayerful understanding you seek should only go as deep as is necessary to keep your attention on the person and work of Christ as he engaged those around him and as he desires to engage you.

To slow the process down and avoid slipping into the habit of reading at your normal pace, it can be helpful to briefly pause after each word before going on to the next one. As you do this, you will break out of your usual reading pattern, and you will make room for silence and careful listening. Your goal is to disrupt the typical frantic pace of life in order to be attentive to God, as you would with your most intimate companion.

As you begin to gently respond to or converse with God about your encounter with him, you'll be ready to move on to the next step.

 Key Questions for Reflection: What does this Bible text say to me? How does it apply to the circumstances of my life? Where is God leading me or what is he revealing to me? What is God asking of me?

STEP THREE: RESPONDING

As you are drawn into a particular passage, begin to converse with God about what you are reading, and seek to respond with your heart. Remember, God has revealed himself as a mystery of personal communion, a unity of Divine Persons. In the Gospels he revealed himself in and through his Son, who lived and died as a full expression of his humanity and his love for you.

Thus, your conversation should be as natural as it is with someone you deeply love, respect, and desire to know better. In whatever manner you are led, based on what you have reflected on or what comes to mind as a result of your prayerful reading, you can ask for forgiveness, you can thank him and praise him, or you can ask him for the grace to be changed by what you have read. You can ask him to help you more fully realize what he wants you to be, and you can ask for his help in applying his moral, spiritual, or practical guidance to your life.

As you engage with him, God may choose to call you to go deeper; you might become lost in a heavenly dialogue with him that moves beyond words. If you tend to be very talkative in life and prayer, it might be important here to minimize your own words and be attentive to Christ and his movements in your soul rather than focused on what you want to say. From here you may find yourself being drawn by God into the next step on this ladder to his heart: resting.

 Key Questions for Responding: What can I say in response to God? Should I offer thanksgiving and praise or should I ask for his help in any particular way?

STEP FOUR: RESTING

Allow yourself to become absorbed in God's words as he invites you into a deeper kind of prayer, one that will bring you into his presence in ways that purely mental exercises could never achieve. You may not experience this kind of absorption as you initially explore this method of prayer. It can take time to get familiar enough with the process so that it fades into the background and becomes a normal expression of your heart. Regardless, God will give you exactly what you need, even if it is not what you desire or expect.

If you give yourself to God in this way he will satisfy your ultimate thirst, your deepest needs, as the Holy Spirit prays with you, in you, and through you. Sometimes you'll be able to recognize this work in your heart; sometimes it will merely be a matter of faith that God is with you, imparting his life-changing grace to you. However, you can always be sure he is at work within you as you seek him in prayer. He has promised that his Word "never returns void" (Isaiah 55:11), and as St. Paul says, "Faith comes from hearing the word of God" (Romans 10:17).

Given that this phase of prayer is not always tangibly sensed, be careful to manage your expectations. In fact, for those who are more advanced in the interior life, it may be a time of dryness and a dark silence, or a simple place of wordless, imageless peace. No matter what, we know by faith that God is true to his word. If you seek him, you will find him, even if he is found in ways that are difficult to understand or very different than you anticipated.

 Key Questions for Resting: Am I being patient, attentive, and open to God's movement in my soul as I rest in his self-revelation?

STEP FIVE: RESOLVING

This final step involves making a clear resolution so you avoid a dangerous trap in the spiritual life: encountering God and doing nothing in response. One of the great spiritual masters of the

Church said this about how we should respond when God reveals something to us in our time of prayer:

> When you rise from meditation, remember the resolutions you have made, and, as occasion presents itself, carefully reduce them to practice that very day. This is the great fruit of meditation, without which it is not only unprofitable, but frequently hurtful: for virtues meditated upon, and not practiced often puff up the spirit, and make us imagine ourselves to be such as we have resolved to be. This, doubtless, would be true if our resolutions were strong and solid; but how can they be really such, but rather vain and dangerous, if not reduced to practice? We must, therefore, by all means, endeavor to practice them, and seek every occasion, little or great, to put them into execution. For example: if I have resolved, by mildness, to become reconciled with such as offend me, I will seek this very day an opportunity to meet them, and kindly salute them; or, if I should not meet them, at least speak well of them, and pray to God for them.[2]

To give an example of my own experience with this step, I was once confronted by a pastor who told me that I was lacking in

---

2 St. Francis de Sales, *An Introduction to the Devout Life* (Dublin: M. H. Gill and Son, 1885), 56–7.

love for others. Coming from a broken background, I was already very aware that I often fell short in my interactions with those around me. I asked him what he recommended I do to improve the way I interacted with others. He suggested that I memorize 1 Corinthians chapter 13, in which St. Paul so clearly reveals what love in action looks like.

As I memorized and repeated these verses over and over again, one day I broke down. I was confronted, in a very practical way, with the reality of how much God loved me and how little I reflected that love to others. Verse 7 was particularly impactful: "Love bears all things, believes all things, hopes all things, endures all things." The more I reflected on this passage, the more I realized that I didn't really understand what love meant in the context of hope.

I discovered a dictionary definition that resonated with me— it revealed *hope* as a "joyful anticipation of good." I reflected on this in prayer and asked what God might be saying to me. He revealed to me that if I loved someone, when that person encountered me, he or she would have a sense that I joyfully anticipated good from him or her. This was deeply convicting for me, since as a natural introvert, I rarely exuded this kind of outward sign of my love for others. My practical resolution was very simple. I made a commitment to outwardly demonstrate my delight and appreciation for others whenever I came in contact with them, particularly those with whom I struggled.

To make this commitment very practical, I determined that I would smile and demonstrate a welcoming tone of voice each time I encountered others for the first time in a given day.

The impact of my encounter with God and the graces he provided through my resolution profoundly changed the relationships in my life.

 Key Questions for Resolving: What can I specifically do to respond to what God has revealed to me in this passage? How can I carry this encounter with me into the day to influence how I think and act?

A QUICK REFERENCE GUIDE
FOR DISCOVERY PRAYER

To make things easier for you, here is a simple guide for you to use for your daily prayer until it becomes second nature.

Reading: An attentive, slow, leisurely, and repetitious reading of a short passage of the Bible

Key Questions: What does the Bible text say in itself? What did the author intend? What does the Church teach about this subject?

Reflecting: Prayerfully engaging with the meaning of the passage and considering how it may apply to your life circumstances

Key Questions: What does this text say to me? How does it apply to my life? Where is God leading me? What is he revealing to me?

Responding: Conversing with God about the passage

Key Questions: What can I say in response to God? Should I offer thanksgiving or praise, or should I ask for his help in any particular way?

Resting: Allowing yourself to rest and remain absorbed in the words of God, allowing or inviting the Holy Spirit to draw you more deeply into his presence through what you've read

Key Questions: Am I being patient, attentive, and open to God's movement in my soul as I rest in his self-revelation?

Resolving: Allowing the encounter with God to permeate your day, causing you to draw ever nearer to him through his self-revelation and invitation to participate with him in making his presence known in the world

Key Questions: What can I specifically do to respond to what God has revealed to me in this passage? How can I carry this encounter with me into the day to influence how I think and act?

Write down your resolutions and conclude with a prayer of thanksgiving.

To sum up Discovery Prayer: Reading *seeks*, reflection *finds*, responding *engages*, resting *tastes*, and the person who experiences an authentic encounter with God *resolves*.

SIX

WINNING THE BATTLE OF PRAYER

The *Catechism* reveals that prayer is a battle. It is a battle against the world, the flesh, and the devil—all the things that seek to distract us from our pursuit of God. This battle takes many forms, but there are common challenges you can expect to face as you seek to draw near to God. For every challenge, though, God provides a way to overcome.

These challenges are easily understood from many angles if you picture your mind as a gigantic tree filled with thousands of noisy monkeys. The monkeys represent everything that distracts you during prayer: your memory, your will, your emotions, your desires, your frustrations, your sins, your shortcomings, your interests, your habits, your good thoughts, your bad thoughts—all that makes you who you are. The number and variety of monkeys usually reflects our age. The older we get, the more we learn and engage in life, and the more we sin and fall and learn. For our purposes, you can assume that you'll gain at least a thousand monkeys for every year of life!

At least initially, none of these monkeys can be trusted to cooperate with your desire to pray. In fact, they will more often incite one another against you, especially at the beginning of a new habit of prayer. The good news is that there are proven strategies you can employ to deal with them. These strategies represent the culmination of thousands of years of wisdom revealed by those who have fought and won the battle of prayer: the saints and mystics of the Church. Of course, I don't recall any of them reflecting on monkeys per se, but many of them shared their challenges with distractions and the ways they overcame them. Here are some practical strategies that will help you deal with the vast majority of monkey business.

Trick Them: The first strategy—and one of the most important—is to trick the monkeys. Many folks who have made progress in prayer have learned that early in the morning, many of the monkeys are sleeping or groggy. When you are working to develop a new prayer habit, getting up fifteen to thirty minutes early can be one of the most challenging but effective ways to mitigate monkey business. Groggy monkeys rarely raise a ruckus. However, once you engage with an iThing or some other kind of electronic device, or when you interact with too many people with too many words, the monkeys begin to wake up and then proceed to wake one another up with a multitude of noises and interests. The tree comes alive! Therefore, one of the most successful strategies practiced by everyone I have ever known who has a deep prayer life is to get up earlier than the monkeys and avoid any engagement with electronics before you sit down to pray.

The secret in two words: Start early.

Tolerate Them: You will have rowdy monkeys in your head until the day you die. Even when the majority of them become holy or obedient, they will always have many interests that surface whenever you turn to God in prayer. In the best case they will attempt to interrupt your prayer with good ideas—holy ideas. In the worst case they will bring to mind self-centered images and thoughts or remind you of past sinful behavior. Regardless of where they come from, the key here is to avoid self-condemnation or frustration. If you allow yourself to become frustrated, this will become a distraction on top of all your other distractions! Even worse, frustrated monkeys will always seek out other disgruntled monkeys that are ready to pile on and distract you even more. When you find yourself distracted, the best practice is to simply and gently turn your thoughts back to God. Even if it takes a hundred times in a half hour, don't be discouraged. Thirty minutes of gentle but persistent turning back to God in prayer is worth more than a half hour of undisturbed bliss in which no exercise of self-discipline is required.

The secret in three words: Learn to relax.

Focus on God!

Train Them: Training monkeys requires outlasting them. You should be encouraged to learn that because of the way God has designed our minds, it only takes about thirty days of consistent effort to get at least a majority of monkeys on board with a new habit or prayer program. That doesn't mean that they will leave you alone after thirty days. But after a month or so, your body begins to expect prayer and will even draw you to it. As is true when you're developing any new habit, the first thirty days will likely be some of the hardest in your journey. The world, the flesh, and the devil are all arrayed against you. Even so, God is greater than these forces, and if you cooperate with him and get up every time you fall, you will find greater success than you ever imagined possible.

The secret in two words: Be persistent.

Tame Them: Monkeys are, by nature, both good and oriented toward mischief. Taming monkeys is a task that takes a long time, but significant progress can be made with one important strategy: Feed them with transformational truth. Feeding monkeys books about prayer and the spiritual life will motivate them to help you in your new prayer discipline. The food they require in order to become docile comes from your participation in the sacraments and prayer itself, but it also comes from the writings and lives of the saints. When the monkeys see the great fruits that emerge through the efforts of others, it increases their desire for this fruit, and they become more comfortable with and desirous of prayer.

This secret in three words: Follow the saints.

Transform Them: When monkeys have been fundamentally transformed (not just behaviorally changed) by their immersion in the truth, they actually become actively helpful in the pursuit of holiness. This transformation comes about through 1) regular and attentive participation at Mass—no less than every Sunday; 2) regular participation in the sacrament of penance—no less than monthly; and 3) daily prayer and a life lived for God. These monkeys *can* be tamed and will work with you to draw your heart to God whenever you desire.

This secret in eight words:
Allow God to transform your heart and mind.

SEVEN

EXPERIENCING GOD IN PRAYER

In my work with thousands of fantastic Catholics at Spiritual-Direction.com and the Avila Institute for Spiritual Formation (Avila-Institute.com), it is very common to see progress in prayer thwarted by false beliefs about God and about ourselves. These false beliefs can come from our upbringing, our self-talk, bad catechesis, and suggestions from the enemy of our souls. Often these false beliefs can be overcome when we encounter truth, especially *the* Truth, Christ himself. This liberating encounter with truth can come from Scripture, tradition, the *Catechism of the Catholic Church*, the lives and teachings of the saints, and the testimonies of ordinary people who are working hard to orient their lives to God.

Other people's stories can be very powerful; they help us realize that we are not alone in this battle. We gain wisdom through hearing about the struggles and successes of others who are very much like us. The following are testimonies of the impact of Discovery Prayer so that you can be encouraged and see what God can and will do for you as you seek him.

Maria, age thirty-five,
married stay-at-home mom with three children

What motivated you to begin praying using Discovery Prayer?

I have been a Catholic all my life, but I never really developed the habit of daily prayer. I took a course on prayer at the Avila Institute, and that made me aware of my need to pray, but I had yet to make a commitment. Then came very painful struggles and heartache in my family that motivated me to seek God in a more serious way. One of my children has gone seriously astray, and as a mom I began to feel that I failed my family because of some of our struggles. It became very clear that only God could help us, and I knew that I needed to learn to pray.

How much time are you spending in prayer every day, and what time do you pray?

I'm just starting out, so I'm taking baby steps. Right now I spend fifteen minutes praying each morning. I am not as disciplined as I would like to be, but I usually pray around 7:00 a.m.

Has this commitment been a struggle for you?

Yes, I have struggled. My spiritual director warned me that

this is common and that it happens to everyone. I've realized that I don't need to worry about my failures but just keep my commitment. If you are on a diet and have one bad day, it doesn't mean you give up on the diet. You just pick up the next day and keep fighting to keep your commitments. It's the same with prayer.

How has this prayer commitment impacted your life?
It is hard to describe. It has given me peace—it's a peace that comes from relying on God to show me the way versus me trying to find a way to help my family on my own. It is also very encouraging to pray—I've seen that I am not alone. I've actually discovered things in the Bible that have helped me realize that my struggles are not unique. God has helped others, and he will help me.

Can you relay an experience that might help others to understand how God has met you in prayer?
Well, I decided I would read through the Gospel of Luke first. One day I read this passage:

> Therefore I tell you, do not be anxious about your
> life, what you shall eat, nor about your body, what
> you shall put on. For life is more than food, and
> the body more than clothing. Consider the ravens:

they neither sow nor reap, they have neither storehouse nor barn, and yet God feeds them. Of how much more value are you than the birds! And which of you by being anxious can add a cubit to his span of life? If then you are not able to do as small a thing as that, why are you anxious about the rest? Consider the lilies, how they grow; they neither toil nor spin; yet I tell you, even Solomon in all his glory was not arrayed like one of these. But if God so clothes the grass which is alive in the field today and tomorrow is thrown into the oven, how much more will he clothe you, O men of little faith! And do not seek what you are to eat and what you are to drink, nor be of anxious mind. For all the nations of the world seek these things; and your Father knows that you need them. Instead, seek his kingdom, and these things shall be yours as well. (Luke 12:22–31)

I am stubborn, and I tend to worry too much. As someone who likes to control things, reflecting on this verse made me realize that I have to let go and let God guide me and my family. As I read these verses I felt a burden lifted off my shoulders. I didn't have to worry about

everything! The frankness and straightforwardness of
Jesus made it clear that God was directly speaking to me
in that moment.

What has been the greatest surprise to you in practicing this prayer?

I was skeptical about the need to pray at a certain time
every day, especially in the morning. I am a night person,
so I assumed that praying at night would be best for me. I
was surprised to discover that the only time I could pray
effectively was in the morning when I was a bit tired and
distractions were at a minimum. My spiritual director
warned me this would be the case, but I didn't believe it
at first.

What is the most encouraging or delightful aspect of this approach to prayer?

Surprisingly, it is two things: First, using the Bible has
been very enjoyable because I am discovering how much
wisdom it contains. As a child I knew the Bible was
important, but as an adult, I am realizing how relevant
it is to us today. Second, the accountability process with
my spiritual director keeps me honest and on the right
track.

Marlan, age forty-seven,
married corporate executive with four children

What motivated you to begin praying using Discovery Prayer?
I had a powerful experience with Christ that resulted in a serious life change for me. When I began reading the Bible daily, I was confronted with the idea that Jesus prayed and admonished us to pray. It seemed to me that if God himself needed to pray and was clear that he desires that we should pray, I should learn how to pray.

How much time are you spending in prayer every day, and what time do you pray?
Well, I am very busy, so I don't pray nearly as much as I would like. I travel quite a bit and have international responsibilities. On top of that, I care very much about caring for my family by my presence. So right now I am only praying about twenty minutes a day first thing in the morning.

Has this commitment been a struggle for you?
Without a doubt! I have accomplished a lot in my life, and I'd like to think I am good at getting things done. That said, spiritual growth has been very challenging to me simply because of my schedule—and maybe because

spiritual growth & intimacy with Jesus

& Mary

of my ego. Even so, it is clearly the most important thing in my life, and I really see it as something where I must be all in—Jesus was all in for me, and I can't do anything less. I can't overemphasize this. Jesus gave everything for me. My life was very dark before Christ. He rescued me out of that darkness, and I don't ever want to go back. I need to pray every day to stay connected to God and the sacraments.

How has this prayer commitment impacted your life?
Immeasurably. I can't say enough about the change in my heart and mind. The level of peace that I have in the face of significant challenges is quite extraordinary. If you would have told me a few years ago that I would come to a place of seeing prayer as indispensable, I would have thought you were some kind of religious fanatic. But now I am committed to yielding my life to God in every way I can until I see him face-to-face.

Can you relay an experience that might help others to understand how God has met you in prayer?
Recently I was drawn to use the Discovery Prayer method with the psalm reading for the Mass of the day. The passage talked about God leading the psalmist to still waters of peace. As a bit of background, I had a difficult childhood,

and one of the few times it was peaceful was when I went fishing with my dad. As I read these verses, God revealed to me that he was present with me in those times and that my peace was a gift from him—a brief place of rest in between the challenges I was facing. It was a powerful moment, and it actually brought me to tears. It is clear that God has been caring for me all of my life, even before I responded to him in any meaningful way.

What has been the greatest surprise to you in practicing this prayer?
I didn't expect to actually experience God's presence. This is probably the biggest surprise to me. Most of the time my prayer time is not filled with fireworks or any feeling at all. I am fine with that because I know I am honoring God and he is working in me regardless of how I feel. That said, I am grateful for the times God has revealed himself to me in very powerful ways.

What is the most encouraging or delightful aspect of this approach to prayer?
It is incredibly powerful to actually have God meet you in prayer. I know I shouldn't expect this, and it may only be a temporary encouragement to me, a consolation. That said,

his presence in prayer and the way he is changing my heart and mind is nothing short of extraordinary.

Erin, age twenty, single student

What motivated you to begin praying using Discovery Prayer?
I wanted to deepen my prayer life. I also wanted to learn Scripture—I wanted to love God more, and I knew that I could do that through Scripture.

How much time are you spending in prayer every day, and what time do you pray?
It depends. It usually takes at least twenty or thirty minutes, but I don't notice the time passing. Sometimes I get lost in prayer and lose track of time. I use my iPhone alarm to help me get to class on time!

Has this commitment been a struggle for you?
When it was first explained to me, I was frustrated and struggled a lot. I was really hung up on getting it exactly right and was worried about not praying correctly. I gave up pretty quickly. Then I went to a conference where it was taught, and it clicked for me. The presenter said,

"You don't have to be working the whole time." I am very action oriented, so this simple statement helped me a lot. I sensed the Holy Spirit telling me to relax.

How has this prayer commitment impacted your life?
It's definitely helped me to create more of a reflective interior life. Recently I was praying through the Gospel of Luke where it says, "Mary pondered these things in her heart." It was sort of an invitation to develop a deeper prayer and interior life. I realized that I needed to be like Mary and ponder the truths of God in my heart. This is one of the reasons why I love this kind of prayer. It keeps the Word of God in my mind and heart every day, and the Holy Spirit reminds me often of what I have read and prayed about.

Can you relay an experience that might help others to understand how God has met you in prayer?
I was recently in adoration praying. The phrase "Blessed is the fruit of thy womb, Jesus" came to my mind, from the beginning of Luke's Gospel. I realized that, just like Mary, my role in life is to bring Jesus to the world. This brought clarity in my own discernment of religious life and gave me peace that if I focused on bringing Jesus to the world, I would be on the right track.

*What has been the greatest surprise to you in practicing
this prayer?*

How much the Scripture comes alive. I came from a good
Catholic family; we are used to hearing Scripture at Mass,
but we don't engage with it ourselves. It is so different to
take the time to really understand what God's message is
for us. Scripture is alive—it's not just something ancient
people wrote and just left there. The Scriptures are the very
words of God. They are alive, and they have the power to
change us.

*What is the most encouraging or delightful aspect of this
approach to prayer?*

It has changed the way I approach everything. I go about
everything in a more contemplative way. It is easier to
make my life a sacrifice; God reveals himself in Scripture in
a way that helps you know what he wants from you and the
way he wants you to live.

Diane, age forty-five, married professional

*What motivated you to begin praying using Discovery
Prayer?*

I am a member of a group called the Apostles of the Way.
We dedicate our lives to prayer and service to others. Part

of our participation is making specific prayer commitments. I began to search for material, and my spiritual
director recommended this approach to me, so I made a
commitment to mental prayer.

How much time are you spending in prayer every day,
and what time do you pray?
My prayer time seems so brief. Right now I spend about
fifteen to twenty minutes each morning. I really wish it was
longer, but my schedule is a challenge. My goal is to develop a solid habit of twenty minutes every day.

Has this commitment been a struggle for you?
At first it was a struggle because I was attempting to fit
prayer into my schedule. As I wrestled with my failures to
pray, I realized the problem. I needed to schedule prayer
first, and then schedule everything else around my prayer
time—just as we do with weekly Mass.

How has this prayer commitment impacted your life?
As I learned to pray, I began to understand who I really was
in relationship to God. This revelation was both very painful
and very beautiful. At one point I had a true revelation of
my sins and the pain they caused Jesus in his suffering and

death. This sorrow drove me to a general confession which revealed God's great mercy and gentleness. Since then I have an abiding peace that permeates my days. My faith has grown, and worldly matters have faded and are of little importance to me. My love for my husband and my family has grown exponentially, and I have a deep desire—though I don't always follow it as well as I should—to treat people with great charity and according to their dignity in God.

Can you relay an experience that might help others to understand how God has met you in prayer?
My encounter with Scripture in prayer has been more of a constant, gentle molding, a greater awareness of God, and a revelation of who God has called me to be rather than any big moment. But God has revealed himself to me in very powerful ways through Scripture. Even though I don't have big moments, I've had a million small but powerful moments. Daily he says to me, "This is the way; this is the way; this is the way."

What has been the greatest surprise to you in practicing this prayer?
How deep the well of grace is, and how empty the promises of the world are.

What is the most encouraging or delightful aspect of this approach to prayer?

The most delightful aspect is how light his burden is—how light the load has become. The most encouraging aspect of this prayer is the strength and peace that it has given me.

Hannah, age nineteen, single student

What motivated you to begin praying using Discovery Prayer?

I was first introduced to this kind of prayer in my junior year of high school. Later a FOCUS missionary helped me to become comfortable and interested in this approach to prayer, and I began to make it a part of my regular prayer time.

How much time are you spending in prayer every day, and what time do you pray?

I pray when I get up before I get ready for the day. I usually spend twenty to twenty-five minutes—on a good day thirty minutes. I really love this time every day.

Has this commitment been a struggle for you?

Yes, definitely. I think it is more of a struggle when I'm at home from school and going to work. It's hard to have that accountability when I'm not surrounded by a community of people my own age who basically have the same mind set or practice. I have to work harder when I am at home.

How has this prayer commitment impacted your life?
It really has helped me to grow closer in my relationship with God. If I keep up a good daily prayer routine, I learn more about God and where my relationship with him is going. I can see when I am off track and when God is wanting to change things in me so I can better love and serve people he has put in my life.

Can you relay an experience that might help others to understand how God has met you in prayer?
Reading the Gospels has helped me to envision myself in the moment with God. Recently I read the passage in John where Jesus was talking with Judas and revealed to him that Judas was to betray him. I realized there are times that I am like Judas and betray Christ with the choices I make, the attitudes I take. When I fail to pray daily, I am really stealing from God. He has given everything for me, and I need to give him my heart in prayer on a daily basis. I feel like it's not fair to God if I don't give him that time every day. Moments like these in

I am shortchanging God by not praying!

Scripture are very powerful to me and help me to better respond to God's call for my life.

What has been the greatest surprise to you in practicing this prayer?
The biggest surprise has been sharing Discovery Prayer with other people and hearing what they reflect on in their prayer time. I lead a weekly Bible study, and when we do group reflection together, it is very powerful to hear others encounter God in prayer. This helps me in my prayer and in my faith.

What is the most encouraging or delightful aspect of this approach to prayer?
For me it's going through the insights I received on the previous day and looking back and seeing how God is working in my life. It's really beautiful to see God's presence in my life.

It is progressive day by day what God says to you. Just listen and believe.

FINAL WORD OF ENCOURAGEMENT

BE SCRAPPY

M y father was the oldest son of a single mom who had next to nothing. He never graduated from college, but he made his first million by the time he was thirty. He also owned two homes by then. He retired at age forty-five.

I learned a lot from my dad growing up. One principle he worked hard to teach me was to be "scrappy." (*Webster's* defines it as "having an aggressive and determined spirit: feisty."[3]) This scrappiness has also translated well to developing a healthy prayer life. I am by no means perfect, but I have found that to the degree that I rely upon God and pursue this principle in my life, success follows. What do scrappy people look like? Here are a few characteristics as they relate to spirituality:

They are positive. Every obstacle they encounter is simply an indication that they need to find a way around it. Often obstacles are due to opposition, and this may reveal that they are on

---

3 *Merriam-Webster*, s.v. "scrappy," http://www.merriam-webster.com /dictionary/scrappy.

the right track. When they know they are being opposed by the enemy of their souls, they are encouraged and thereby redouble their commitments to God.

They are resourceful. No matter what the obstacle, they never stand by helplessly; instead they immediately begin to look for solutions. By the grace of God, they almost never fail to find solutions, even if those solutions seem to be incomplete or imperfect. The key is that they never give up until they achieve the goals they are committed to. God always rewards the resourceful heart with wisdom.

They are trusting. They know that God is in control, and that every obstacle is provided for their sanctification. Knowing this, they are confident that God will help them to overcome, and they know they will learn from their failures. As they trust God, he responds by encouraging them and giving them the strength they need to persevere.

The have a long view. They know that sometimes answers don't come in the short term, but the most important things in life are often only attained after long toil in the right direction. With this powerful perspective in hand, short-term challenges never discourage them. They recognize that as long as they remain with God, he will see them through.

They are resilient. They never give up when it comes to the most important things in life. Resilience is the ability to be flexible and adaptable. This attitude translates into docility with

submission to God

God, trusting that although it may be uncomfortable and require change, God will never ask more of them than they can handle; he will give them what they need to answer his high calling.

They are consistent. They get up every day and engage in prayer, no matter how they feel or what else is happening in their lives. They recognize that God can't help someone who refuses to engage every day. *Ask don't beg for help*

They are humble. They are quick to seek help when they can't seem to find a way on their own. They recognize that they don't know everything, and thus they regularly seek the counsel of others. They know where their strength comes from—they know they are weak and incapable of making progress on their own and that the source of strength and real solutions can only come from God. They believe that God always delivers on his promises.

Yes, prayer is a battle. Battlefields are no place for the half-hearted, but for those who are willing, the battle will be won. Yet sometimes we just don't have the raw material to get started, or to get unstuck. Being scrappy implies that we have a good understanding of the domain we operate in. We know the right people; we understand the resources available to us.

In the realm of prayer and the interior life, most Catholics have never been given even the most basic formation regarding how to successfully navigate the interior life and grow in their relationship with God. This book, of course, is a fantastic start. To further help you in your adventure, the following resource can help you continue your success in the journey to God. If you are ready to get scrappy in your prayer life, there is no better time than now. Be scrappy, my friends, and you will know a joy and peace that you never thought possible.

RESOURCE FOR THE ADVENTURE

To reward those who have made it this far,
we have created a free video mini-course on prayer!

Go to www.SpiritualDirection.com/Pray
and use the code DISCOVER.

*Are you looking to continue to deepen
your faith and relationship with God?*

SpiritualDirection.com can help!

SpiritualDirection.com is a website dedicated to supporting you on your spiritual journey. If you visit and become a subscriber (it is free) you will find:

- Daily or weekly emails that will provide you with encouragement and insights into how to deepen your relationship with God. These will come in the form of videos and blog posts.

- Notices regarding exciting online learning opportunities and courses on prayer, discernment of spirits, and many other topics.

- Invitations to events or webinars that will no doubt inspire and uplift you as you seek Him.

- News of new books and materials just like the one you hold.

We hope you will join us there!